# Far From Home

Books by T. Alan Broughton

Poetry

*In the Face of Descent* (1975)
*Far From Home* (1979)

Prose

*A Family Gathering* (1977)

# Far From Home

poems by

# T. Alan Broughton

**Carnegie-Mellon University Press**
**Pittsburgh and London 1979**

*For Laurie: Home, wherever you are*

## Acknowledgments

Acknowledgment is made to editors of the
following magazines in which most of these
poems first appeared:

*The Attic, The Beloit Poetry Journal, Cedar Rock,
Cincinnati Poetry Review, Confrontation,
Descant, A Flowering After Frost, Four Quarters,
Jam To-day, Review La Booche, Lakes and
Prairies, Northeast, Poem, Poetry Now,
Poetry Northwest, Three Rivers Poetry Journal,
The Virginia Quarterly Review,* and *Yankee.*

The following poems were first published in
*Poetry,* CXXXIII, No. 1 (October, 1978):
"Grace," "Inhibition," "Happiness,"
"Loneliness," and "Fear". Copyright, Modern
Poetry Association.

"Faunus" and "Hold, Hold" received Emily
Clark Balch Awards from *The Virginia Quarterly
Review* in 1974.

Library of Congress Catalog Card Number: 78-74989
ISBN 0-915604-25-6
ISBN 0-915604-26-4 Pbk.
Copyright© 1979 by T. Alan Broughton

# Contents

IV   In Deeper

V   Creation Songs at Forty

VI   Three Voices: Delphi

# I   The Interference of Blood

# The Lesson

All for the sake of art
you left me there.
Those unscuffed shoes,
the unaccustomed tie,
and forelock damply kept back from my brow
were preparation for the sacrifice.
Her cave was walled
with pictures of her demons
(Bach in his surly wig, Beethoven grimly disheveled),
perfumed by brew that bubbled in her teacup;
and black-boxed like a fallen harp
her instrument of torture
grinned its mottled teeth
where for a trebled hour
I flinched my fingertips among dark tongues
that thrust to trip me up.
Behind me that evil stepmother hovered
while whole notes split to halves, to quarters,
to hemi-demi-semi-quavers of panic.
And yet I learned that witch's magic
and soon became apprenticed
to worlds beyond your gentle knowledge.
Mother, who once abandoned me,
the price we've paid for such desertion
are all these songs
I conjure up from practice,
the wild notes flung that set to words
the space between us.

# My Father Dragged by Horses

Beyond the yard the barn is hulking
and somewhere behind my shoulder the women
are kneading and chopping their way to lunch.
Into this sun-pressed waiting
the horses come slowly, slowly
dragging the harrow where my father rides,
reins binding him over the gleaming disks.

He turns to wave
and horses sensing the slip of mastery
bolt for the pasture. In a jolt
he is thrown and bound,
arms stretched suppliant
to unleashed hooves, his body
dragged and the knives spinning,
spinning and waiting for straps to break.

Somewhere out of my sight the horses
feel his body still holding on,
and stop, mouths flecked with bloody foam,
stamping as my father rises,
wrists deepcut by thongs; and the knives hold still.

Again and again in the slowest of motions
they advance from the right
and my breath is dragged out.
This is the rhythm of every nightmare:
lovely precision of danger held in check,
rider in harmony over the animal and honed device,
and then the fall, the utter descent
to flailing hooves and a hundred sharp suns.

# Moon Eclipse

Your hands that shook me out of sleep
were the pale reach of a father
who owned the boy stalking my dreams.
All windows leaked gray light
and things were not as they should be:
cherry trees bloomed dust,
the sidewalk was a sluice,
your lap was slate
and breath slid by my ear
to blow out the moon.
The pipes knocked once.
Your voice explained the sun.

Now  another night bleeds
through its distant wound.
Voices in a city street wear masks
beneath my window, and I sit
and wait for darkening.
Far behind me
a woman breathes in our bed.
The smoking chimney of a neighbor house
is the mocking gnomon of my time.
We've walked on the moon
and trod it down
and no one holds me now.
I own a child
who sees the crisp edge of my flight;
my hands shake only air
where there is nothing to forgive.

The ball you threw too hard
rolled under the bushes
and we gave up looking for it.
Your skin burned at the beach
so you stayed home.
I think in a dark night
I saw you walk in circles on the lawn
and would not let you hold me
when I woke from bad dreams.
Always the light was behind us.

I watched the backyard sink.
The house of gables faded,
all flowers turned black.
Obsidian as Egyptian statues
we waited for doors to swing.
I felt the hinges in your heart.
I slept

and woke to this dream, old father,
where an alabastor disk
like webbed fingers held to light
shines with the interference of our blood.

# Naming the Changes

At first we spoke,
but when the road washed up and through the headlights
tugging us into our own split worlds of silence,
we let ourselves be children in our darks,
let single words repeat
like keys against stiff tumbrils,
*mother, father* chanted out of sense.

Hands on the wheel,
were you forward, already in the blind,
ducks wheeling from the blade of ice,
or back in grief for your mother's death?
Always remembered pain begins its flight
across the corner of the eye
before it can be named.

I thought of how
hunting comes from a father,
how he loads, gives your shoulder up
to its first shock under his eyes,
hands showing hands the way,
until the trigger becomes his finger
touching yours.
But mine was a man of soil,
turned ground or pages,
did not stalk beyond his fence,
and I will never share
the blood of beasts we might have killed:
the wrenched neck,
feathers blown across white earth.

Your face grew unfamiliar,
masked by the dashboard's glow,
your eyes as blank
as when you passed me
going to the funeral—
you, your father in the front seat
and prim driver of some limousine
bringing you to a parlor
trite as all common grief.
I could not forgive a windshield
that glazed me from your face piked and stern,
moving to a mother coldly waiting
beyond words in the deep trench
of silence.

We knew the signs that took us north,
but even the road seemed strange.


II


We lugged the engine to the boat,
broke water black as earth
to drop decoys in the sky.
Like lumpish twins we stood in the blind,
shifted our weight in search of warmth
and small waves lost their motions under us.
Your words were directions
given too late to help
the awkward way I lifted hands
unused to the brush of cedar,
unable to trust the space you knew by heart.
*Father*, the mind's tongue said in gall,
and black shapes bobbed just out of reach.

You never mentioned her death except
one night at my house
you spoke of giving your mother up,
that savage choice of hospitals:
the breath turned off,
her white face closed,
and child in a corridor
weeping like a man.


III

Reeds are scratches,
water breaks from sky.
Somewhere away shots send a thousand geese
crying from a bay,
shards of our land,
and night drains out
in a flutter of wings
too far away to shoot.
Our lives go watchful and apart
as if the first light centers our sorrow.

Where in this water
has your heart sunk to?
My father sleeps
but dreams across my blood,
turns restlessly upon my mind.
I plow the furrow in a marsh,
fish eat my seeds,
I cannot shoot that flock.
Is *mother* your cry?
The stroke she took
is a knife that slips
across the block.
The print is flawed.

Men in their blinds
are shooting at the dying night.

IV

Trees give up to light.
Rocks are not water,
water is bright and pulling the reeds.
One wounded teal
swims in and through our flock,
nudging the indifferent bulks.

Through unmarked air
I plunge a hand.
Your arm is a hold
I climb back to myself.
Your face again takes shape,
the features of a life beyond my own.
Back from the river
we cannot cross, we come,
geese in the shape they need
move on, and when you speak my name
I know I am.  Love for this moment
does not need to understand.

V

We killed no ducks that day
but plucked the decoys from the cold
and drove home on a mundane road
of oiltrucks and the names of towns reeled in.
Our sorrows strange under the sun,
we doubled back,
voices wing to wing.

*for bill davison*

15

# Apple Wine 1975

We have cleaned old bottles
making them our own,
have stood them shining
in neat rows.  We lugged
the gallon jugs to the table
where gently I release their locks,
dipping the siphon through the crust
that gathered in months of quiet working.

You kneel ready
to hand the bottles as I fill,
not knowing the taste of wine
or even willing yet to try.
Maybe when these come to term
you will be avid as your father
for whatever respite evening brings.

All weekend we have spent together
in woods, walking gingerly
across the last crust of snow
where water cut hollow passage
under us, and once when I slipped
you warned me to take care.
My thirty years beyond you,
dangerously folding to dimness,
are sometimes struck by undertones
of a single note, the deep blow
of the lake's first crack in ice;
and now I watch you come of age,
each day a season on its own,
but each caught in the lag
before some knowing lifts it into light.

Maybe years from now
you will remember the layered flurries
hiding the river from us,
the pale sun barely warm enough
to let us sense that winter had turned.
Keep what you will of our passing —
the wind that cuffed us, plucked our breath,
the icicles you shattered for pure sound —
or any moments gathering from your birth
to different ripeness than I know.

You hold the bottle up.
I draw, my mouth fills
with raw and skittish wine,
and we watch its pale gold
veil the glass. We will cork
and label all these rows
then lay them in the closet,
stacking the dark with waiting.


*for camm*

17

## Out of Touch

The leaves, a pink dress on the neighbor's line,
are turned by a balmy wind
into gills, floating and valved.
Such evening air is salve for the coming
of a sleepless, humid night.
I think you do not close
the windows of your distant house
even if thunderstorms are expected,
and you have returned
from cobalt treatment number five.
*Salve regina.*
Neither of us knows well
how to pray.

We twined out of shared childhood,
twisting up the same stone face
until some trellice parted our ways.
Now I climb down that vine
to see the giant eating at our roots
and cannot kill him.
We slid from the balcony,
went to the woods and played with fire,
we danced and burned the trees,
touched each other's naked bodies
on the far corner of a grass-eaten tennis court,
skins eggshell smooth and first flames lifting
under the brittle surface.
We let fireflies trapped in jars
ignite dark corners of our room
while a whole moon washed our dreams.

One breathless night you came to my room,
already your breasts half-gathered,
reaching out to wake me,
and I held your pulse in my palm,
we stared at each other,
you whispered *what*
*shall we do*
*what shall we*
*do* until my father hearing strange noises
in his night, tramped down the hall
and you hid under the bed.
Soon you ran from all of us,
grew past stepmother
away to a husband and sons and distrust
of this snobbish, distant cousin
who coveted all the family's worst madness
while your blood went slowly more berserk
than anything I've done.
Perverse cells, one-eyed,
rage across your helpless land;
they have no terror of my words
and further down than memory
eat and eat.

Elizabeth, captive queen,
the stories we read say
I can take a hatchet to the vine
and all the evil tumbles down.

But there is no safety in that —
kingdom, leaves of our doings,
hinges and beds, sprouts
falling inward with one rush.
If you die I live on
like the victim of a stroke,
tongue numbed and heavy.

Part of the flaming fabric
folds back in this gentle breeze
and does not unfurl again to sight.
I believe in currents,
in the flow made visible
by the small shaking of leaves,
the gathering of water into clouds,
and believe in the kingdom of the unseen —
but would not lose sight of you.

Always time seemed of no consequence
except as metrics to our song.
Yet now I sit and spread the oldest balm
across our wound,
words,
and then the singing stops.
Cicadas pause in air that ripens into rain,
fireflies fold darkly, again I cannot hear
your breathing, and this is where I fall asleep,
holding you as I always held you,
in my mind.

# II  Stolen Pleasures

# Toys

The best were for the bathtub,
not the guns
or things he pedaled or roller skates
that could not negotiate
the hiccups of pavements
flinging him to knees and scabs

but toys for tubs:
those fishes filled
with floating colored spots,
the sequined ducks,
boats he harbored in his crotch
or sank on an iceberg of toes.

How devious the ways to cleanliness,
demands for finer things:
the PT boat that ran on soda
sputtering through suds,
the submarine that dove
and whirred on the bottom
heard only on skin.

But always the best was beyond
his reach in the costliest store:
the diver's suit with leaded feet,
a stiffly rumpled cloth
and hands as mutely spread behind the glass
as the face of the plaster boy
who took his place
where he should have seen the water masked,
the long cord trailing from his belly
back to all his needs,
hard head cleaving
the new-wet world

where he would have drifted
beyond the fish or even into stars,
wide eyes swimming in the light
and hands unclutched.

## The Thief of Films

Going in or out is dangerous.
The street screwed to its afternoon light
is a groove any parent might take.

The lady scoops his stolen quarter,
whirs the ticket, stiff as God's tongue
out of its trap.
What does she care,
this keeper of delights,
that the coin was lifted
screaming from a mother's purse;
and the ticket taker is bored to shreds.

He hunches in the middle seats
and prays for dimming.
Beyond the ceiling's light
fringed like a hip with shattered baubles,
the pink-cheeked Titaness stares —
too early, too early.

The curtain sucks itself in.
Next week's possible sin is displayed
and he clutches his knees
falling, rolling
past Batman
past the lion's mouth
into the vast black and white of loneliest pleasures,
fearing the end when with a rush
he is swept out,
eyes blinking with rejection
          of common sun
          of concrete anyone can walk
          of the long arch toward next Saturday

when beggared hands will grope for coins,
blind as roots.

# The First Kill

He rolled the copper beads down the barrel.
No reason to suspect them.
Red Ryder had done as much on his horse,
hi-ho and away.

He cocked to the groin,
slung one shot at the sun
and pumped again.

On a pine branch the bird
warbled a resinous air.
Blueberries grew by the swamp
and a trigger is all for pulling.

Its throat turned amber
and he kneeled in bush and bramble
to stare at the saffron beak.

This was a piece of the sun
that had learned to sing.
What was left was only a feather.

## Laces

Alice Hawkins is tying his shoes.
She stoops and he looks down
on the broad neck and shoulder
flat as a yoke.

"You see how easy it is,"
she says, but he is not watching
her stubby fingers.
Loudly her companion argues
with his father over Cicero.
"You only need to make
two bows, two small wings
and tie them together like this,"
says Alice and looks up
to see his eyes blank
as a stone head of Caesar.

Now when he bends to tie his shoes
he does it like no one else.
He does not know Latin.
Alice Hawkins has flown up
from her drooping flesh
and utters only gerunds.
How did he learn to make this knot
without looking?

# May Day

The Maygirls dance to their poles.
The fire brigade has volunteered
to come with their instruments,
marching behind.
                Each girl carries
her basket of daffodils
nodding their heads
like wired curls.
Their college blazers cover
the breasts, of all shapes cupped
in diverse brassieres.
                Wilting
forsythia and cherry blossoms
border the quad
where professors inspect
the student beauties
prancing in unison to the poles.

These are his maidens.  He is nine,
the prince of faculty brats
come for his visual *droit du seigneur*
to stand by the bushes,
each one blooming in his mind.
Oompah, oompah
is the rhythm they follow.
                He doesn't know
why he watches or what
in the lifting of their hems
as they skip
keeps him there until
the school bus takes him off.

They still jig past.
Pyromaniac of desire,
he would flame under each thigh.
Loose the alarm,
let the Band scatter
back to their ladder trucks
and high roof acts.
Give him one moment
alone with the tuba.
He will dance them round and round the pole
until they melt like tigers,
his lilies,
sweet butter that he spreads.

# First, Love

They lurk in the basement of school,
take turns being first to arrive
in a room where all the sets
of forgotten plays are stored.
They have their parts by heart.
He is the Prince returned
through claws, flesh scarred
by the guardian dragons of recess,
and she is newly awakened Lady-of-
they-know-not-what
but her rising-falling chest
and pale grip of chalkdusted hand
show her distress.

Never touching lip to lip
they stare for fifty minutes, stare
at the eyes that vaguely fear
the impossible reach to come
when they will kiss and kiss
lips raw on the frozen mouths
of lovers trapped in some icy moat.

Out of that heaped storage room
again and again her face shines up.
He leans to kiss
but their bent light
sheers off.

## Past the Garden

He walked that lane to school,
became expert in all its weathers:
            hard earth under pebbles in late Fall,
            precise location of puddles,
            and various journeys of vines
            before some gardener clipped them back.
It crossed a lawn below a dormitory,
took a coy dip between a row of maples,
passed a broken arbor
            where always his foxy mind smelled sex
and hugged at last the high wood wall
beyond which (O the knotholes let him know)
was the slate-splashed garden of some goddess,
            its fretful iron-work of chairs,
            white mosaics of a tabletop,
            lilypads defining water and sky
an impossible place.
He never saw a human there
who touched a single chair or flower.

Last night he returned in sleep.
Out of his burned house
only one sink remained,
            bleached sunflower
            stuck high on its plumbing.
The cat crouched in the cinders and laughed.
No one slept in the dormitory
and out of the arbor his father sidled,
            back half-turned
            while he wiped his mouth with a rag.

Before he could place his eye to the hole
the wall flamed open
and white as burned asbestos she came,
              greenhouse smell lush before her,
              click-click of her evening shoes on stone
and she gave him shimmering in his hands
a white rabbit that he cupped to his neck.
All memory trembled in its pulse.

What could he do with a rabbit?
He could not keep it fed
or give it proper care.
He let it go,
opening his hands in the wide fields
far from home.

# III   Leaving the Clearing

# For the Feast of the Immaculate Conception

Mary in your garden
mother-to-be and
frightened to find a
stranger with his wand
who kneels when
you were only there
to read a while
I love you

in all your trans -
formations
        Umbrian
landscapes or trees
no one can believe in
or the much too rich
brocade and silks
you are
beneath such praise
as naked as
I see you

perennial as a
sonnet
you hold the fruit
of holy plucking
a breast released
the babe sometimes
an old man in his face
or fat or playing with
a bird
      but always
I know you

for the face you wear is
the face we dream
to quiet us from
the worst of nightmares
or the touch of hand
that wakes us
from our sweaty sheets
in dark rooms
              to turn
away the blank gaze of
the hawk-faced god
I need you

do not shrink so
your slim hips
bowing away from
the angel's touch
              your
one hand held
as if his wand could
burn
       no matter how
you did conceive
I take you

Mary
     your bare breasts
firm as apples
no driven rending
in your rites
        I will
be gentle in my
love and send you
now this touch
that grows white wings
throat downy with
white
    my dove
that flies to you
and nestles in
your thighs
      whose gift
of love will follow on
a winter's night.

# No Ithaca

Dawn and another island.
Beyond its fringe of foam
she bends and motions with the wind,
her voice blown back
through the gathering trees.

Is she the one I left
before memory congealed?
I think there was a roof
sloped as that one is,
and now that I see her long hair
catch the glint and spray,
I'm sure she has been waiting like this
since winds that shifted blew me off.

Somewhere behind, the child I am
steps on each stone of island
one by one
and hears laments, the bitter twists.
Was there a war, a dog, a nurse
or did I read that once?

I love two women and have left them both.
They stain my dreams
                the color of moon shadows.
They tumble and coax about me all the night.

Their cries at the moment of coming
                are not the same:
one moans like the hinges of earth,
the other is the most delicate bird
                that sings in a flight of gold.

Their breasts are as different as two landscapes
and when they speak their words cannot be contained
                in the same score.

All my life they will sing
back to back.

# Seven Lyrics for Absence

## I

I walk to your fire.
Often the other women are waiting
but you are taken.
I circle the block
or stand in the arch,
watching the stars move on.

I am not jealous when Fiat or Jaguar
drop you down the street.
The hand that waves them off
returns to your hip.

You know me and I know
your fee.  Each night I hold your face,
water cupped in my hands.

## II

I see your face in the window,
turn quickly
but glass shifts traffic, myself, and chrome
into a cascade of objects
gleaming through moss between us.

I'm sure your eyes are there—
they blink, lips part to speak
but my face thrust close
dissolves into the darkened store
with single light hung
far back in an office
and carved chair whose arms
are held out stiffly.

## III

That night I pay for all your hours.
Our loving done, we sit
on the bench in a dark piazza.
Delicate hands in your lap,
through weariness you take delight
in a thumb-nail moon pale
above the heavy cornice
of some palace, and as it rises
a white planet follows
over the low cantle of its flight.

When the sky is soaked blue
we rise shivering and walk
as closely as we can
to the earliest café to open.
With coffee bitter in our mouths
we go to our beds.

## IV

You do not bring
the jangling glare of diversion.
Your jewels are quiet,
the passage of stars.
How lovely the rustle of falling clothes,
your long hair drawn across my face
as you arc like a white bow
above me. Your love cries
are the small lap of waves
the wide sea breaks in mid-ocean.

Out of the sound of your breathing
in sleep, I have learned
the wisdom of silence.

V

Even if a pig is born with five heads,
a woman gives birth to a monkey,
or showers of bees cluster
the head of Marcus Aurelius,
I will not stop climbing
the five flights to your bed
near the window.

Only true prodigies
prevent my going further:
the door locked,
someone else's voice
inside.

VI

Because I am late I take a taxi.
One week before, I left your bed
at dawn while you still lay
in sleep, dark hair like a cat
stretched over the pillows.
You had wept when I entered you
and not told why.

The city always works against us.
I wait for a funeral:
its scrolled glass catafalque with wreaths
and limousines of mourners, pale
faces set in black.
When I reach your flat
the door is locked.

Are you inside clenched in anger?
Do you hear my footsteps
as I descend? Or is there
only furniture, blank
as your shuttered window.

## VII

Tonight I cannot sleep
and rise to watch
a moon tear back the clouds
and lie naked in sky.

Soon I return
through gauze curtains
smelling lightly of dust
and enter my bedroom.

The moon is soaking
the rumpled sheets.
It might have been you,
for only a moment slipped
out of my bed.

## Cornucopia

Such outrage of fruit
when the early sun
cut its wedge on stone:
the carts in pyramids of
apples golden or red-seared,
persimmons split,
their juices spread
to yellow-banded wasps,
heads of lettuce
profligate in leaves,
pale lemons, figs

we could not hold it all
when the dog ran loose
and Sergio the boy dove
upsetting the cart
and we were all hands and feet,
up to our ankles
in scurrying fruits
where drunk bees hummed,
the old man raved,
until our square became a bursting fig
the sun had riven

and we laughed out of
breath in the dark stairwell
all the way to bed,
our shoes stained and slick
as we threw them off
and clasped each other,
naked tumblers.

# Relief

One day sun-burnished as a bowl
we walked the Via Appia only intent
on being where we were
          and after drinking
our bottle of wine with backs to a tower
disheveled as the burdocked fields,
we ran for the sake of running
into an opening the plow had cleared for us.
Stooping suddenly and out of breath
you lifted a fragment of relief
          a maenad soiled
by her long dance in clay but lively
still
      her plait swinging loosely by her neck,
eyes closed to the rhythm her body once
had beat for her as she whirled
through lines of reaching satyrs
long since broken away.
         But still she danced
and since she lacked companions,
sun and field and furrows under us
completed her motion and we were
flung out in her robes and steps,
the wild flutes playing in our eyes
         dancing with her now
            and now
in all our partial moments.

# A Poem for Waking

In Rome where the surface shimmers
under a sky bluer than credible
and slashed by swallows,
I pay to have the telephone
alarm you from your dreams two thousand miles away,
my voice hurled down through ocean
and wide-eyed fish where the cable twists,
and I surface in your hallway
among cats crying for their food,
where the dog begins its morning
with a circle at your feet.

Out of those waves of sound
you ride on a voice
that in its first breath murmurs *Yes,*
holding us in its echoes.
May I always wake you
with a hand that moves
over a parabola of caring
to the place you lie,
wanting only to be where you rise
from the sea of your long dark
hair flung on the pillow near my face,
your crescent a furrow for the ancient plowing
of water that parts
and folds and parts again,
your eyes in dazed passage

letting the first dawn touch us
as you take me in,
air rippling between us and the old sun
flying to its own erosion:
light in our bodies,
fire held in our hands.

*for laurie*

# The Harvest

Unmarred blue and leaves floating down,
flecks of old sun at our feet,
the brook stippled and dog nosing ahead
to scamper back.
The mind is lost in pure description,
outward bound into the gold
and absolute line of stones,
and the body follows close behind.

The day lifts us up the ridge
and meaning enters wholly
through every touch.  Even the geese
that cry across us from the right
are gapped and wobbling in their order
as if this sun could not decline
but only ripen and ripen.

But we know what they describe,
and when I say *It's over*
you can nod;
and we have no fear
even when we descend
and the shade of the mountain
thrusts us into a cleft
far from that still shining blue,
even when we wake at night
shivering from hard frost
cutting the last green down.
I hold your living hand

## Coming Home

Do you remember how
the house was ours
months before we moved there,
how the others
who had owned it
slept and ate
and played their drums there
and when we passed
how furtively we glanced back
as though afraid
it would sink in a quarry

and that we even forgot
it was ours
until we found ourselves
packing a truck
with trunks and boxes
while friends helped
bundle us in
up to our necks in parcels
of two lives, the bare floor
echoing to our shy footsteps

and we slept upstairs
to turn at times and see
the shadows mark strange walls
and hear a new dog barking
until we woke in the trees,
birds singing in our air.


*for bonnie and ted*

## Leaving the Clearing

We could not tend the trees
without first cutting down
the growth of stout saplings
choking our orchard.
But as I buzzed and hacked
and you hauled limbs away
more apple trees appeared
stealthily huddled far up the slope.
We saw this could be
the work of years.

We had to choose the best,
give up the rest to maple and pine,
to foraging bears and deer that snorted,
reaching from haunches up
through heraldic necks to the fruit.
Next there was brush to scythe,
the tangled alders at each base
hiding the rock that chipped
my blade into sparks.

Finally we clambered with saw
and clippers into twined branches,
so lost in the overlap
that often we cut twice at the same shoot
or felt our perch sag us
downward, sawn away
by our own bewildered hands.

We will never know
if each year's harvest has increased.
We left each other and that place.
I forgot a hand-saw which must swing now
/ rusted on the stump of a long-healed branch.
The alders grow back, water sprouts bristle
the unkempt forks.
I think of deer each fall
standing at last light
on the edge of our dwindling space,
wary of such openness but lured
by the laden branch,
the gathering fruit that casts its tang
far in under birch and pine.
I think of how we would wake
in that cabin on the first night of snow
and hear the barred owls
work their barking way in hunt
up the long valley, into our dreams.

For some seasons the apples
will burden those trees in profusion,
and even years from now,
as long as each tree stands,
their trunks will bear the scars of what they lost.

# IV    In Deeper

# Return

Wracked all day
the woman has been the long way down
and up again on her donkey,
pounding the clothes on rocks,
numbed in the noon daze of sun.
She rose before the birds woke
and at night can barely speak
to her man, watching her hands
do their last motions before they drop
like rocks at her sides
and she sleeps.

All souls bend back to their weary
task of animation
and bodies they take move on.
Nothing explains this remorseless return.
But the things of beauty
travel with them:
her whorled hands
and eyes whose carved lines
cast nets of kindness.
The sea still labors in her blood.

In midday, in the heat of toil,
somewhere near Naples a voice sings
and words fall out of air.

## Hold, Hold

We lay still
        our two worlds
laced as hands
when you said *look*
and we watched a mouse begin
a strange descent
along the piping to the lamp.

We could tell by the way
he paused
to close his eyes as if
pain took him in his gut
that he had taken
poison we'd set out.

           Naked
I rose and fetched a pail
a lead pipe
        nudged him into it
started to bear him out
when you said *maybe*
*you should drown him.*

           It was
kindness to fill the pail with water
watching his fur go sleek
as he tried the slick sides
not a sound as he paddled
all of it held in the black eyes
not even looking at me
           but deeper into
the swirl of all things

and then I held him under
with pipe against the side
his feet jerking
small bubbles and a spot of blood
issuing from his nose
      and myself held
in the steel sides
our chalice brimming with ripples going out
into shivering grass
the trees bending away
birds suddenly flying back
hawk in a plummet
      its strings
cut
and all that night the stars
wheeled angrily like motes
in a muddied spring
      where I am
getting in deeper
in deeper in
deeper.

# Trophy

I wanted the bones
his head threw out,
rack of his lust.
What would he care
long dead, the table
where carrion snouts
and beaks had gorged
with leisure, course
by course.  I turned
the stag by its horns,
unhoused the layers
of maggots and worms
pale in their indolent
sucking to bones

and caught in the updraft
of his rot I hung
petaled in flesh
stem and marrow
stamen that flags
collapsing inward
on its juice
           both of us
flowers of motion
upright or fallen.

Bearing the horns home in my car,
I own the monument,
stone roots of his rutting,
and still some taint adheres.
I open the window,
pass the farms and breathe
the shit, the felled hay,
earth in heat.

## Perspective

a child crying
late afternoon
it might snow
someone's car
won't start
he's through trying now

who is it
whose child
why don't they
do something
the leaves still
hang on the oak

he stands far out
on the iced pond
in a snowsuit
a redwool cap
he is facing
away

there are no other
kids with him
why does his sobbing
hurt me
not his father
not even his friend

I can see the ice
has been cleaned
where he is
where are the other
children what
is that he has dragged

over the snow
that has blurred
his own tracks
left a furrow
he is silent now
in the bare space

the sun is falling
red behind the swamp
the pines are black sticks
the drowned pines
are bones
of the broken land

we are staring
at the same thing

I am weeping now.

# How to See my Death

You barely stir as I rise
in early morning when light lies only
at the foot of the bed.
By the time I have dressed
you have turned once
and lifted far enough to the surface
to see me waver in the doorway,
then I am gone.

The first birds skitter from the feeder,
the neighbor's cat who has stretched
from sleep to waking lust
slinks in the wet grass.
I begin my run
flicking pebbles, letting
the stride fall short
as muscles wake and green begins
to flow around me — bush and tree
and lilacs clutched in their cones.
Breath mounts in me, my heart,
old thing of checks and flaws,
tries to find the measure
of this new tide

and you have reached your bare leg
into my place, letting that vacant touch
wake you to the limbs
of trees, a crazy robin scolding
at the roof and plummeting moon.
Rolling the covers back
like a loose-lipped wave
you lift your knees,
breasts and small veins purple as the sea,
then put yourself in clothes.

Now I am turned toward home,
feet kicked out and legs
taking lengths of a road I knew
until the last turn where old apples
twist and writhe to find a bloom
and she stands in an upsprung wind,
sea-foam scudding from her hems,
eyes of the cave where moon
sleeps into day
                    and my heart
with home in my eyes
breaks in a surge,
dives in the drown of its blood,
my hands out to clutch
once more at this world
where cats sing the stalking bird
and you in your yellow harbor
mend the nets.

They will carry me back as if dead,
lax hand and sweat turned cold.
But this old face lies
in its dull repose.
Look.  I still run
where field holds its ragged edge to sky,
her hair flung darkly,
and she has me by the hand,
new roads rising
to our touch and go.

# Faunus

## I

There is a door into woods,
a path where trees open out
to heights, and leaves in sun
are stains of light.
He walks into its nave
full of wet speakings,
sees the south wind
flapping the peels of birch,
the hill's edge sailing out.
Against that tree's wet belly
                    he unreels,
coils arms and legs
to her pendent arch.
               Ferns quaver
as he greenly thrusts.
They share the bright
translucence of the seed.

## II

Love turns as he turns.
The deer of quiet eyes
              neck bowed
to the apple fallen in goldenrod
has gathered the dew of ferns
on whitened belly.
             The buff sides
heave with gorging.
She has borne no fawn
has crossed the fall woods
              only to
the distant click of bone,
the brow of mates.
He leaves the trees,
sun washing on his thighs.

                                        Her head
lifts
and ooze of cider still pressed
on her startled tongue
                             she droops,
neck and legs spraddled
to his touch of tip
and flange down to
its balled root
                   master
of loam.
                   She staggers under
his swipe of heat against
fall leaf
              gray and naked nights.
She buckles and takes
and foams at his cast.
                             The bees
are drunk on all their juices.

III

Now by the bank
                        he tumbles
weaves feet splashing
stone sloshed
                   shoulders and hips
nudging the banks.
                             The fallen apples
bob and turn
                   stems and puckers
of release.  He swims
                             wades,
the stones' skins moiling
over the bubbles of sun
                             his feet
in slime, hands paddling, spreads
and he falls into tumble of shadows.

Minnowing pebbles are
flecked to his coming.
In his channel he rides
the last roll with eyes closed
                    brushed
by alder and willow,
plunges to pond and salamanders,
lolls as she lists
             and kisses
her banks
        the shudder
of muscles down the sheer flanks,
her watery fingers in all his crevices.

IV

He floats in scales of wind
tugs at the passage of moon,
lets his breath bear him over
her needs
         the silt and sift.
Dragonflies sew him to
clouds
      he turns to hands that knead
his back and buttock
            she reaches
her palm to his breastbone
              he breathes
and dives, lost in her bell,
in unfastened rollings and tucks.
She in her silence
unfolds.

V

Out of the woods
                    out
of the water out
of the sun's and moon's ramble
he comes
            to be creature.
Where shall he wander
                          kissed
by what women
                    how
shall he cease
                thighs
always burdened?
                    Into
the long boats,
down to the scarfing rocks and shale,
driving his sheep to
the one-eyed caves
                    what city
can founder or
                    bricks hold
the vine as it clambers.

## Under All Seasons

I watch the slow resolving into spring,
fierce reluctance of pocked snow.
Those humps in the neighbor's yard
are only abandoned cars, wrecked hopes
of failed mobility, and bare vines
that will turn them into clumps of green
are twisted cords binding them closer
to a clenched, scoured earth.
These days I shield a fragile wish
against the shattering of the sky,
air again torn to white shreds —
season when even the flash of cardinals
cannot delight.

Too often in my own gray room I become
a weary emperor on the Danube
writing back sad resolutions against
the violence without, the whirl within.
All of my age, bombed from the air,
from underneath even in deserts,
from the smallest envelopes delivered in the mail
lies strewn, jaw-broken, wordless
and I hear a black river tearing under ice,
all our brothers turned to stone.

What have I written down
that stays for even a moment
that rending of wind or hand?
Once it would have sufficed
to name the turnings, to say
*The sun will come closer,*
*that bare tree already shifts its sap*
*and gathers to burst in green fire.*

But I know at night such blaze turns black
and under the tree some woman will lie
hurled down, her own clothes stuffed in her mouth.
Not the old opposings, hate against hate,
anger for anger, can redeem this time,
or any flight away to hover above the tent
to see myself hunched on a camp stool
in a flickering light in a field by a river
in a night on the world in a whirl of planets.

I look for the lasting simple
we have always known,
all things conspire to hide.
Under the crust-cold years
or tentacles of suspicion for the worst
it does not change, born with us
all along when hands, bewildered,
found it webbed in our touch,
when words meant to cut
were blunted by kindness.
A father's hand that holds the whip
falters, his face cannot stay clenched
and if his fear of what the child must learn
lifts his arm, he will tremble in the silence
of his own dark room and come to stand by the door
only to listen to his breathing son.

Silent, unbroken by the river gnashing
ice floes over bank and rock,
lost to our sight shocked by the sheer extremity of blood,
it stays.
I name you now,
I give you this poem of thanks,
word more durable than pain:
gentleness.

*for douglas worth*

## Planet Dream

rising through sky
the center of blue
                    turned
without falling
                    breathing
the light
          no stars or moon
and arms outstretched
                    my legs
akimbo
          whirl on whirl
is this water or sky
shapes and folds me
                    I am
full of blue
          naked
my skin wet
                    my new
eyes
     hips and wheeling sockets
I am turning, turning
                    trees
rocks and rivers rise
from my fire
                    white arch
of bone
          fingers and tongue
rolled forever in blue
water and air
                    plunging
layer on layer

# V  Creation Songs at Forty

# I   The Creation of Fear

Even the way the horses chew
scares him.  When their huge hooves
strike down in their stalls
he shies away, in danger
of backing into tools or machines.
The hay loft has holes, traps
hidden by bales, and to doze there
would bare him to rats.

One night a thunderstorm shakes
every board of the house.  From his bed
he glimpses trees flung out
like stripped umbrellas.  Birds
strike the house, fists of windy rage.
In the morning he runs to see
the calf that strangled
in the gate to its stall, head
thrust through the slats in fright.

They disengage it.
When they drop it into the wet hole
the body doubles up and farts.
One cousin laughs,
and all afternoon pitches the baseball
at him so fast his hands swells up,
but he stands there for hours.

That night, while the house sleeps,
he feels the dead beast settle
in its field, and he cannot hold off
the hard white light that whirls
toward his face.

## II    Loneliness

He prefers to play alone.
They won't believe him,
think him queer, and worry.
*You should have friends*
*You should learn to play with others*
*You shouldn't skulk by yourself.*
At night he can hear them
on the other side of the wall:
*He should go to Jimmy's house*
*He should talk to someone his age*
and their old bed shakes and beats
against his room.

He tries to quiet them,
spends the night at Andrew's house
and throws up on the floor.
No one is as fine a D'Artagnan
as the man who springs with rapier full-drawn
out of his head.  The old bush
by the corner of the house supplies
the sword he flourishes, turning
to parry and thrust against the source
until it is so stripped of leaves
it dies.

Inside they brood over his fate.
Out of their fear they fashion
a little man to keep him company:
its eyes are the windows of old apartments
on Sunday, and voice is the rasp
when a telephone rings him
out of sleep, he lifts the receiver,
and no one is there.

Now he and his companion
live together in their own house
and imagine each other.

## III    Sex

The submarine wears out.
He loses interest in amphibious planes
or the volcano of his knee
pushing up through soapsuds.
He begins to look with curiosity
at the body of his sitter.
As she bends to tie his shoe
he curves to the loop of her shirt,
or when she stoops to dress in the dune
he lizards up the slithering hill.

He decides they ought to take
a bath together.  She smells
like his mother's soap.  He cups
the pink cake in his hand,
slides it on the only part
so far wasted.
She is vaguely there unfolding
further and further to his plunge,
her body as close as water.

In all her forms she rubs him into shape.

## IV   Inhibition

He is playing the black coffin.
Its keys grin and try to bite.
When he looks up from Beethoven
his mother stands at the far end
of the room on a dolly,
and then she rolls up
over the bare oak, hair disheveled,
eyes struck with grief.

She carries letters,
the old sheets of his first love,
stained by his thrust and groan.
The creak of slow wheels,
the sawing hands with their fluttering packets
raise a new kind of music.
Through the falling serpents of her hair
she hisses *Promise O*
*promise me that this*
*won't come to pass again.*

He shakes his head
but his groin turns to stone.

# V    Restlessness

He never realized he could come apart,
assumed the hand was tied
forever to wrist and arm.
The first day he slips a finger
under Anne's door and leaves it there.
She doesn't seem to mind.
But Susan lives three miles away
and he has to pedal to her house.
He plants a foot in her garden
where parents won't find it
and lopsides home.
There is also Roxanne and penny-breasted Deborah
and an unpronounceable blond
he knows as *Runcible Spoon*.

After a while he hasn't much left
for himself.  He decides
to call in his parts.
But they don't come.
He digs with his stump in Roxanne's garden
but finds only a dead cat,
lifts the hem of Deborah's skirt
to a passle of giggles.
They've all forgotten his gifts,
say *Shoo shoo* with their hands
and move to different cities.

## VI   Love

He wakes to a wind
that rushes down the night
as if it falls from flooding stars
to shake the trees and swing doors
in whirling eddies.  No light,
and even his breath is snatched out
to some tattered world beyond him.

He does not know his age
or where he is,
hears the earth plunging into space,
seals of planets cracking,
his own cells scattering, never
to gather in one place again.

No wonder a sheer
joy of light takes him
when the storm has passed
and in the first check and fault of sight
her sleeping face appears,
composed and known.  He reaches,
and his body comes together in a hand.

## VII    Happiness

One day he loses everything.
Not a fire, not confiscation.
He simply can't remember
where he put them.

His shirts hang loose without cufflinks.
His car door is locked forever.
American Express sends huge bills
for things he does not possess.
His children are waiting
to be picked up in towns
whose names he can't recall.
He walks into class with his fly open
and does not even remember
to be embarrassed.

*Well,* he says, *well well.*
Suddenly he remembers that it is
not important to remember.
He laughs and laughs.

## VIII    Irony

The first time he looks in the mirror
he is certain it tells the truth.
He is all eyes, and the collar
his mother has bent to his neck
almost smothers his tie.

Later he keeps sneaking back
for a glimpse. He learns
at sixteen to turn one mirror
to another so he peers
not at himself, but away,
languidly. For the first time
he notices his nose.

At thirty he learns when to look
and when not to.
The person who uses his eyes
for peepholes is much younger
than that eroding billboard.
But still he takes his teeth,
those whorled ears,
seriously.

On his birthday at forty
he raises his hand
with razor to his cheek
and observes the image
has not obeyed, does not hold
an implement other than a finger
which it points at him
and with barely perceptible grin
begins to snicker. The lips split,
the wrinkles converge.
Only the face in the mirror
is laughing.

## IX    Grace

He is in a place
where there is nothing to do all day
but lift small stones
that keep rolling over his legs.
They have grown smooth
with the touch of his fingers.
For as far as he can see
there is only slate
and the small hump of a grinding machine
on the rim of his pit.
He has forgotten thirst.

Toward the end of that year
he decides to talk to the rocks
in their own language.
*Chuck, chuck. Padunk. Glock.*
No answer. He remembers an old joke.
The next stone he picks up
he calls *mother*. The next is *father*.
He gives them both a *bird*
and tosses them over his shoulder.

The grinding machine stops
to listen. He is getting excited.
*Eyes*, he shrieks. *Garden.*
*Carburetor.* Toward nightfall
the stones have begun to line up
for names. They knock together
and chuckle. On the seventh morning
he lies back and listens
to their deepthroated
hymn of praise.

# VI    Three Voices:  Delphi

# 1.

I am the voice of the boy
killed by wandering shepherds.
My father spoke
with the words of a poet,
his friends came with him
onto the mountain, Parnassus,
over the shrine of Apollo,
and snow was still high on the peak.
I was seven
and my body was clear as Parian marble,
my eyes green as the ripening olive.
Why did we go?
I was never told
except I know how my father
believes in old myths
and his friends believe in his words.

They chose a high camp
on the ridge where the bay swept out
from rocks beneath us,
and jumbled ruins clung
like shattered wisps of an old eagle's nest.
The sun sank into our campfire.
I heard their voices
in the circle of dark,
my father lifted up parts of songs
in the old tongue and then lapsed
into his own before I wriggled
and faded like a spark into my dreams.
How could I know what would await me
when I woke at dawn
and left them sleeping among tilted bottles
to walk over ridge and gully,
looking only for a sight of the summit
my father had promised we'd reach that day.

They were stooped in a circle,
backs and vests of lamb's wool turned to me,
so at first I thought them animals,
expected the bell-wether's startled face,
but found only masks of wild eyes
and their hands on my arms,
and still I was not afraid
because these were like the poor men
of my father's island,
the ones who live in stones and gorse
and talk to their sheep and gods.
They did not treat me roughly
for I was the answered prayer,
the wandering image of Dionysos
the mountain had given them.
When my feet bled in the long path
they lifted me up
and took me on their shoulders,
and the old one who walked beside me
touched my thigh
as if I were sacred glass,
the chalice of flesh.

High on the ridge
near the edge of snow
they piled rocks for an altar
and whetted the knife in my presence.
I wept and struggled
when they led me up.
I was cold when they took
what clothes I had.
How could I understand
the gentle reverence

they touched all parts of me with,
or the strange words
they said through my pleas?
With love they raised me up
as if I were newly delivered
from some prize ewe.
The thin blade slit my voice.
I would tell my father
*Live in the sacred body,*
*let the hands that caress you*
*lift you lovingly*
*before you are set down on stone.*

They found me in spring.
I'd turned to bones.
My father no longer sings,
The old gods have fastened his tongue.


## 2.

I am the voice of the place.
I speak for the almond trees
and the eagles.

We blossomed here long before
the coming of altars.
In these twists and curvets of stone
the sun is always drawing us out,
coaxing our flowers into
the welcoming drone of the bees.
Before they came we cast our fruit
in profusion into the tufted weeds,

and the wild goats grazed at our feet.
In one place for all these years,
in one place watching stones hewn out,
white marble outshining our petals,
the bleating of sacrifice
while earth, that drags at our roots
and eats what we drop,
drinks itself black with blood,
we have watched the ground devour those stones,
the men loose their hammers,
lovers under our boughs fall asleep,
and our honey still flows in one place
fixed between sea and sky.

We rise on our still wings
only on what we sense
in spread sinew and feather,
and lifting in circles from perch to perch
as the sun draws the air up ino itself,
we spiral toward our golden hole in the sky
and hear the voice of air,
deep breathing of earth,
up past rough jaws of rock
where we rest and peck
at the split and ruddied fur of the hare,
past the last eddy of cove and cusp
and into the cold river
that flows forever from snows and peaks
till the trees lose their shapes
and the temples are nothing but scars,
the bay is a finger a wide sea jabs
at the land, and we are seven circles in tiers,
our eyes turned now to the sun,
our wings on fire to rise.

# 3.

. . . speaks now
speaks forever
        my voice
the unending river
with no source
        no ocean
of destination
        always flowing
that they may dip into it
with their own vessels,
holding a moment
in the cupped palm
this fragment
        this still
clear song
        Apollon
Apollon . . .

# Carnegie-Mellon Poetry